Mindful thoughts for
STUDENTS

First published in 2021 by

Leaping Hare Press

An imprint of The Quarto Group, The Old Brewery,
6 Blundell Street, London N7 9BH, United Kingdom
T (0)20 7700 6700
www.QuartoKnows.com

© 2021 Quarto Publishing plc

All rights reserved. No part of this book may be reproduced or
transmitted in any form or by any means, electronic or mechanical,
including photocopying, recording, or by any information storage-and-
retrieval system, without written permission from the copyright holder.

British Library Cataloguing-in-Publication Data
A catalogue record for this book is available from the British Library

ISBN: 978-0-7112-6177-8

This book was conceived, designed and produced by

Leaping Hare Press

Publisher: *Richard Green*
Commissioning Editor: *Monica Perdoni*
Project Editor: *Laura Bulbeck*
Copy Editor: *Claire Saunders*
Designer: *Maisy Ruffels*
Illustrator: *Lehel Kovacs*

Printed in China

1 3 5 7 9 10 8 6 4 2

I started to read this book on July 13, 2022

End to read on August 05, 20 22

Mindful thoughts for
STUDENTS

NURTURE YOUR MIND,
FLOURISH IN LIFE

Georgina Hooper

Leaping Hare Press

Contents

The Learning
Journey

Educators will often impress on their students the importance of good study habits. As both a teacher and a life-long learner, I have seen many different approaches to learning, and tried many myself. Of them all, mindful scholarship is the most empowering, effective and gentle. Through many years of applying the techniques of mindfulness, I have opened my eyes and mind to see that there is no single 'right' way to be a student. The path to learning is unique to every human being, and this path must be found through the development of self-knowledge.

The practice of intertwining mindfulness and study is a learning philosophy that cultivates the development of self-knowledge alongside academic knowledge. The object of our attention becomes not just our particular field of study, but ourselves as a learner.

In Japanese and Chinese, the word to represent mindfulness, 念, consists of two characters: 今 meaning 'now', and 心 meaning 'mind'. A mindful approach to study cultivates attention through our 'now mind'. This simply means developing a habit of mentally being here and now in the lived moment. This is achieved by awareness of our bodies, our environments and our mental activity. When we are present-minded, we can worry less about the future, where exams, assignments and presentations loom, and we can let go of the past, where old failures can threaten to crush our confidence. Mindfulness offers strategies for resilience, helping us bounce back and turn up when we are challenged or our motivation dips. It fosters our mental health by building self-compassion, and helps us de-stress by relaxing our nervous systems. It strengthens our self-discipline and ability to concentrate, by training the mind like a muscle. When we integrate mindfulness with study, we equip ourselves with a greater capacity for joy in learning, and build within ourselves the habit of recognizing our achievements through self-observation and awareness.

Mindfulness fosters insightful knowing, rather than a brain overloaded with information. Through the self-knowledge that comes with mindfulness, we can intentionally foster what is beneficial to us and let go of what no longer serves us, empowering ourselves to make conscious and wise choices in our study and for ourselves. As we come to understand the way we learn best, we also come to intimately know ourselves and who we are as human beings, part of both small and global communities.

I am excited to offer through this book the insights I have gleaned on my journey as a scholar, a teacher and a practitioner of mindfulness. The act of learning, when we do it mindfully, can be greatly deepened, and foster in us a love of learning that can lift us up in our lives in ways that we never imagined.

One Step
at a Time

It can seem overwhelming when we start out on
our journey as a student. A mountain of work looms
ominously in the distance, and as we look at the
path stretching ahead of us, and consider the distance
that needs to be covered, we can feel crushed by the
enormity of the task before we have even taken the
first step.

The great Chinese philosopher Lao Tzu said, 'The
journey of a thousand miles begins where you are and
with a step.' Life is simply a
series of many individual
moments strung together over
time. By bringing your focus to

the immediate moment and tuning in to the present, you can be empowered to make strong choices for your 'right now' and take the steps needed to achieve your scholarly aspirations. Small and consistent practices make for big and affecting change. How well we mindfully choose to use each moment often determines the wider outcome of our existence. With consistent attention to the present moment, we have the capacity to reach great heights as students.

SEEING TIME

Reflecting on the time we have as a series of moments can help us break up the larger tasks in our study into achievable and intentional increments. I have always used a year calendar in my study, so that I can see the year before me as a series of little steps. A visual reference to time and the individual moments at our disposal becomes a wonderful way to bring us back to the importance of a well-used present.

When you want to achieve something, consider not the amount of time it will take, but instead what the specific means are for reaching that goal. Once you have determined the incremental steps that are needed, bring your attention entirely back to the very first step. If you are overwhelmed with the idea of starting an assignment, make a map. What seems like such a large distance to cross, from empty page to finished task, can be broken up into a list of small and manageable steps. The simple act of plotting a course to navigate with can help to stop us from feeling quite so lost.

TIME TRAVEL

There is a great deal of uncertainty when we try to project ourselves in the future, and so many variables that it is impossible to predict the outcome. When we bury ourselves deep in thought about the future, envisaging ourselves reaping rewards and achieving the goals we set, we can lose touch with the present and feel discontented with reality, longing for achievements we have not yet attained. When our mind continually returns to the goal of our future, the carrot that drives us is always tantalizingly beyond reach. If our gaze is fixed ahead of us, we can find ourselves doing tasks on autopilot, with only half of ourselves there.

The present moment, however, is fertile ground for us to plant our feet firmly on. Mindfulness, which brings awareness and attention to what is taking place in the present, trains us to be content in the present. We can savour the satisfaction of the things that are experienced fully. We need not rush through the journey in anticipation of its end when we study in a mindful way. The value of the journey is the experience of it.

The fable of the hare and the tortoise is one which speaks to the merit of steady progress. There is no need to rush through life towards another time. Life is lived in the present, and when we move through it at a comfortable and consistent pace, it is surprising the ground that we can cover. Living in the present moment is much like surrendering ourselves to a journey by sailing boat – we can't rush the wind or urge the waves to carry us faster; we can only navigate and direct the rudder, holding our hand firmly at the stern, our attention at the helm. The more deeply concentrated you are on each individual task, the fuller and richer your journey as a student becomes. Your only guaranteed moment is this one, right now, and when you slow down and focus, you are more likely to notice the flowers along the way. By embracing the present moment, we can all move towards living life as fully as possible, one day at a time.

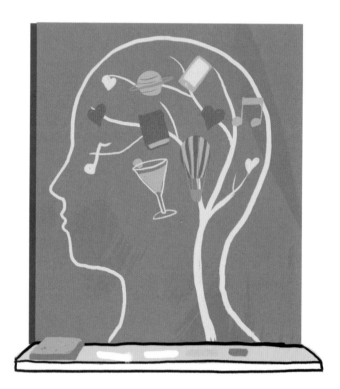

Wandering
Minds

One of the greatest challenges shared by students and practitioners of mindfulness alike is maintaining concentration. Both study and mindfulness primarily require us to consistently direct and focus our attention. But this is not an easy task. Research suggests that our minds wander for 50 per cent of our waking moments. That means that we can be missing half of the content delivered in a lecture, taking in half of what we read and sitting at the study desk for twice as long as we need to.

Through mindfulness we can become more effective and efficient when we study. By adopting a mindful approach to our work, we can tame the wandering mind, hone our attention and achieve better results.

Techniques of mindfulness present wonderful tools and practices for students to grow their capacity to focus in among the constant distractions. Mindfulness practices cultivate an awareness of how distractions work and train the brain to focus regardless of them.

DOWN THE RABBIT HOLE

Distractions can be sorted into two categories: internal wandering, and external diversions. External stimulus can be compelling. Anyone who has ever sat next to their best friend in class can testify to this! The diversions of what is happening in our surrounding physical and social environment can make it difficult to focus on a teacher, book or writing task. Such outside stimulus can lead to a cascade of internal wanderings as they trigger our memory or imagination, leading us down the rabbit hole and away from our study.

It can be difficult to stay out of Wonderland long and consistently enough to achieve anything some days. The mind is a limitless, timeless playground that can take us on endless journeys to the past and future through its internal rhetoric and imagination. There is no end to the distraction it can offer up, and it delivers highly compelling stuff. Our brain is so good at keeping us from being bored that it often becomes the obstacle that stands in the way of us reaching our goals and full potential. The wandering mind will always be there, and external diversions are impossible to avoid, but with self-awareness and conscious choice we can cultivate a greater capacity to concentrate.

ATTENTION, PLEASE

The first step to conquering the compulsion to slip off-task is to simply observe your mind – to pay attention to your attention. It might seem like a naïve practice, but cultivating your ability to notice your mind wandering is both challenging and essential in bringing it swiftly back into focus. Like any skilful truant, the brain will slip away with such stealth that we don't even notice. Quite often we can be well into a daydream before even realizing that we have seriously deviated from the task at hand. Sometimes a whole class can go by in which we have not been present or engaged with what was being taught at all.

Mindfulness fosters a practice of discipline in staying in the present moment. As we practise self-awareness, it will become more natural, even habitual, to catch ourselves in distracted states. Once in the habit of being watchful of our attention, it becomes quicker for us to identify when we are not on-task. This means there is less time away from where you want (or need) to be. By paying attention to the natural inclination of the brain to wander, we can more sensitively understand what is pulling our focus and do something about it.

OBSERVE THE MIND, BE 'IN' THE BODY

We can learn to identify our distractions more intimately by embodying them. This is about tuning in to the physical sensations that accompany our distractions. When you feel your attention wander, ask yourself, 'Am I trying to avoid discomfort, or am I perhaps longing for pleasure?' Maybe your shoulders are stiff from hunching over a computer, or your brain is physically tired from holding itself on a challenging area of study. Or perhaps you are looking forward to the rush of feel-good hormones your body will receive from you checking your social media. Mind and body are part of the same system, and we can enhance our awareness of both by witnessing them operating together.

When we foster our capacity to observe our concentration, or lack of it, study becomes so much easier. Honing one's attention is like playing a game of squash. The distractions come at you from all angles, but in remembering to be aware of your awareness, you take that first step backwards to see the field of attention at play, and in doing so, can develop a game plan for how to deal with them.

Finding Focus
& Flow

Mindfulness at its very core is an elegantly straightforward two-part practice. The first part is amplifying awareness of the internal mind and body, as well as the external environment in the present moment. The second and very vital part of mindfulness is the element of choice that we have in what and where we direct our attention to. This choice is one that is made constantly. In the face of each new thought and every sensory experience, we choose where to point the spotlight of our attention.

In making the wise choice for ourselves as students we are often choosing to tolerate discomfort and boredom or delay the gratification of pleasure or fun. That is the thing about choice: as we grasp something, there is always something that we let go of. With mindfulness, we are making our choices consciously, with awareness and intention. When we make a wise choice for the use of each moment, directing our attention to that which will help us in our pursuit of scholarship, we empower ourselves for success in our study. This might be choosing to wait until the end of the lesson to tell your friend your exciting idea, or refusing to respond to the tantalising pull to check social media on your phone in the middle of writing an essay. But it might also be delaying thoughts about what to eat for lunch, or ignoring the internal chatter about something that happened yesterday, last week or last year. These choices are never-ceasing, but with practice, it will become easier to let the distractors pass by without responding to them.

MENTAL MOSQUITOS

Robert J. Sawyer once eloquently stated, 'Learning to ignore things is one of the greatest paths to inner peace.' This beautiful statement was exemplified for me when in seated meditation during a yoga retreat in Thailand. The conditions for my success in mindfully focusing could not have seemed better but, 2 minutes in, I had an itch. A tickle on my nose, now a hair brushing my face, an annoyance on my arm. I thought to myself, 'Is that a mosquito?' My mind flitted backwards and forwards, contemplating whether or not I should break my pose and brush away the annoyance. But by then I had already lost my focus.

When we sit with the intention to focus our mind, no matter how determined we might be, little itches will want scratching. But the power of distractions often lies in the 'mental maybe' that we allow them. Rather than simply observing the irritation and dismissing it, we 'to-and-fro' with the idea of scratching the itch that plagues us. The mind is like my 4-year-old child: if she thinks there is a possibility of ice cream, she will keep asking for it. The only way to firmly address the tugs of our attention is with a firm and certain 'no'.

A MATTER OF CHOICE

We are constantly faced with the choice to come back to focus. Setting an intention to do so, we are empowered to direct our attention positively. The key is to be diligent in continuing to make the choice to positively focus our attention. As we practise the habit of first identifying that we are distracted and then having the discipline to bring our attention back to the task, we foster a kind of mental fitness and expand our capacity to concentrate for longer. The more we learn to observe the agitations of mind and body and practise resolutely letting them go, the more we minimize how long we are mentally off-task for. Cultivating this resolve and determination to keep our mind on our study helps us go more deeply into what we are learning and can increase our rate of retention.

The funny thing is, once you have set your mind to a determined mindset of ignoring disturbances and longings, they will miraculously go away. Of course, others can pop up in their place, but with practice you can train yourself to brush those disturbances away with greater speed and ease. Once you have become resolute and practised in your diligence to stay present, the task of being a student becomes so much easier.

Mindfulness is about not always doing what feels good. Using mindfulness, we can endure a little discomfort or deny instant gratification by choosing, with conscious awareness, the more distant pleasure of the outcome we seek to attain. For students, this probably isn't enlightenment like it was for the Zen Buddhists, but it might be improved grades, a degree or PhD, or just the phenomenal pleasure of cultivating knowledge and understanding.

For the Love
of Learning

It is all well and good to preach the importance of staying on-task when we study. But this challenge can be made even more difficult when we are simply not interested in what we are learning. Discovering what sparks our interest can ignite in us a passion for learning that puts the wind in our sails on our journey as students. Mindfulness can offer us strategies to discover our passion and help us to foster it.

Discovering what you love is an essential step in becoming a life-long learner. Before I found my passion, I was entirely disengaged from study. As a teenager, I would wake up tired on school days and drag my feet on the way to school, invariably ending up late.

In class, I was uninterested, and my assignments were always thrown together at the last minute. That was until I decided at age 14 that I would become an artist. I became the first to arrive at school, waiting for the teacher to let me into the art room. I was the last to leave at the end of the day, with the cleaners locking up after me. I worked on my art at weekends and was powerfully motivated. I had found a passion for learning.

LISTENING IN

Finding your love in learning is a journey that begins with learning to listen. For some, our passion can flare within us so brightly that we cannot possibly miss it. But for most of us, it is only a faint glimmer in the beginning, a hunch, an inkling that we must watch for, following clues in our life and learning. Mindfulness can help us to see the shining breadcrumbs that illuminate our path home, leading us towards the thing that we intrinsically love.

We often think of study as being oriented in the brain, but knowledge can be found in the body too. Desire, passion and curiosity lead to a sharpening of attention and a surge of energy that can be felt physically if we are tuned into our bodies. In the presence of something good, the brain releases four main feel-good chemicals: endorphin, oxytocin, serotonin and dopamine. If, when we are learning, we are tuned into our bodies, we can sense the physical effects of this chemistry as we experience a thrill of interest in a certain subject. Mindfulness is a practice of observing in the present moment, not just the mind but also the body and one's feelings. It is a path to coming to know oneself, deeply and presently.

THE CALL OF THE UNKNOWN

In mindfulness, we are encouraged to observe the here and now without engaging in judgement. When we practise non-judgement, we remain more open to experiencing our present moment truthfully, rather than engaging with a type of personal auto-correct that fills in for us what we think we ought to be feeling or thinking. What if you find yourself really excited about learning something that isn't cool, or is maybe even a bit odd? You don't want to override your intuitive stirring of interest by cutting it down with judgement.

As a high school teacher of art I often came across many concerned parents who were reluctant to allow their children to take art as a subject. Their concern, that the subject may not lead to later career success, was also reflected by many students who feared choosing the 'wrong' path. When we sense a surge of interest flaring within us, it is important not to dampen it with judgement. A mindful student listens to the call to knowledge and allows it to bloom, without prematurely cutting it down. The path to learning, like the path in life, is full of unknowns and surprises. Quite often, when we follow our passion for study, we end up creating unexpected opportunities or joining together previously unrelated areas of knowledge and expertise.

LEARNING & LIVING AUTHENTICALLY

If we are to procure our brain's constant attention in our studies, it needs to be on board wholeheartedly. If there is doubt about what you really want to be doing or achieving, the brain will respond in turn. Treading a path of study where there is resistance to learning is like trying to sail a boat with its anchor down. The weight of our doubt and reluctance can make the journey to scholarly success extremely difficult.

Part of the journey to living and learning intuitively, authentically and joyfully is learning to hear, listen to and trust the voice within us that whispers of love, fascination and joy. What greater success can we have when we live our lives learning about and doing what we love!

Tests
& the Feedback Loop

One of the realities of being a student is that we are assessed, rated and compared with others to give us feedback on our knowledge. Though this is often unavoidable and is at times uncomfortable, it can also be useful, and doesn't have to be destructive or stressful. While assessment results can leave us feeling deflated and even defeated if we don't get the marks we might hope for, mindfulness can stop us from internalizing and catastrophizing this sort of feedback.

Alongside the feedback of assessment, we may also glean feedback from ourselves, which can bring with it self-knowledge. To gain this insight, we need to listen carefully to what is going on inside our bodies and minds. The practice of mindfulness often refers to focusing attention on an object in the here and now. By making this object ourselves – our body and our thoughts – we can mindfully attend to our reaction, as it happens, when we receive feedback. This is a very useful practice, as receiving assessment results is often a time of heightened emotion. The anticipation we feel is sometimes excitement and sometimes dread. Perhaps we get a test back only to find we failed. In this case we might immediately feel our pulse rise and our breath quicken. This sort of feeling could be described as an 'arousing'.

Arousings are the moments when we shift from tranquillity and ease to an emotionally or physically heightened state. Such experiences, which we probably have quite often, can be considered as the beginning of the road to insight. When experiencing a surge of emotion or a strong physical response, consider: is the feeling pleasant, or painful, or not painful or pleasant? By observing from a distance the reactions of our body, and the thoughts that accompany them, we can cultivate a calmness of mind, and are provided with 'starting points' for a deeper self-knowledge and wise understanding. It is a different kind of feedback than that which we might usually focus on, but it is equally important for our journey as mindful learners.

SELF-CRITICISM & SELF-BELIEF

During and after assessment, you might find that listening in to the rhetoric of your mind reveals your inner examiner. This is your internal voice of self-critique and criticism. How you intellectually and emotionally respond to assessment grades can teach you a great deal about how you feel about yourself, what your expectations are and what drives you in your learning journey. You may find you can be far harsher on yourself than any teacher could ever be. Or perhaps you discover you are so disheartened by your results that you don't feel like trying anymore.

So how do we navigate the treacherous territory of the red pen and emerge from our learning experiences with our self-belief intact? Self-belief has more to do with what happens within us than it does with the external conditions of our study. In fostering self-belief in our inherent capacity to learn, through watchful thinking and mindfulness, we can reduce anxiety and the potential of external examinations to derail us. When you find yourself making absolute statements, such as 'I'm dumb' or 'I'm not smart enough' or 'This mark isn't good enough', try to look deeper to see the relationships between things. For instance, if you didn't do well, maybe you didn't listen in class, or perhaps you need to learn better time management. Or maybe you are learning about something that is really challenging and you just haven't got it yet. It isn't about how smart you are. Assessment is designed to capture what you know at one specific moment in time. Your marks are only valid for a short time, so take what you can learn from the feedback and learn to let it go.

CHECK YOUR EXPECTATIONS

Mindfulness encourages us to cultivate faithful and non-judgemental observations of ourselves and others. It provides us with a certain distance from our emotions and thoughts, providing a buffer and space for us to question what we might otherwise readily accept or react to. When we observe our responses to our assessment results, we can qualify how reasonable and rational our belief systems are.

Listen in to your expectations. What do you expect of yourself? Are your expectations realistic? What unnecessary pressure might you be carrying around and where might this come from? The weight of expectations can weigh heavily on us and cause a great deal of unnecessary stress when it comes to tests and grades. By letting go of our harsh, unrealistic expectations, we can surrender to the natural pace of our growth, which if we apply ourselves with sincere diligence, happens organically.

Trust the
Process

To learn is to walk a path from the unknown to the known. Study will not always be easy. There will be times when you don't understand or don't get it, feel out of your depth, frustrated, lost, may even as a consequence switch off and lose hope. But with mindfulness we can bring clarity to the process and cycles of learning and build our trust in them.

THE CYCLES OF LEARNING

As mindful learners we build self-awareness. As we practise seeing, feeling and experiencing our emotions and thoughts during the cycles of learning, we become familiar with the uncomfortable feelings associated with learning, such as not knowing or understanding something. When uncertainty settles upon you, consider it a familiar friend come to visit rather than a harbinger of doom. We all feel uncertain at times. Building awareness that uncertainty is just part of the process helps us to cultivate patience and endurance. Uncertainty isn't a bad thing, it's just a little uncomfortable. Understanding the cycles of intellectual growth, and identifying them through our familiar reactions, allows us to fall back on our trust of the learning process and remember that these moments are not only normal in our journey as learners, but necessary. We can trust that as we step from certain ground into confusion, we will find solid ground once again.

Understanding the process of learning is to inherently believe in ourselves as adaptable beings that can flourish under extraordinary conditions and adversity. The Buddhist symbol of the lotus represents our capacity to learn, to grow from the mud into something more. It speaks of the human ability to thrive, not just through adversity but because of it; the mud is the sustenance for our development. As students this means that it is the challenges of study, the hard stuff, that help us bloom. Understanding how we ultimately thrive through challenge can help us trust in the learning process.

AN UNDULATING PATH

Learning as a process never happens in a straight line. Success in your studies doesn't mean that you will always move smoothly from point a to point b, increasing your grades and knowledge consistently. Like the rugged path of a craggy mountain, the route of learning is not always a direct hike up. You may find yourself walking down for periods into the depths of the unknown only to have to climb your way out, one precipice at a time. We don't want to lose sight of the details of such an ascent, nor should we hope to avoid them.

I remember reading (or trying to read) Fyodor Dostoevsky's novel *The Idiot*. I found the title completely ironic as I felt like a complete fool reading it. Having been a voracious reader from a young age, I was perplexed by how confused I was – I couldn't follow it at all. The book was the earthquake that shook my self-belief. I stopped reading in disgust and have never picked the book up again. Often on the path to understanding you might find yourself feeling lost or completely confused as I did. It is at this stage that many abandon hope, either by switching off mentally or quitting entirely. These moments of uncertainty can be deeply uncomfortable. Not feeling in control can be difficult. This is totally normal. In the leap to knowledge you can expect to feel a bit like *The Idiot* before you can feel smart or capable. Rather than assume something is impossible for you, like reading Dostoevsky seemed to me, you can seek something to scaffold the leap. Perhaps I could have looked for a study guide to the novel, taken a class on Russian literature, started a book club or asked someone for help.

EBB & FLOW

What is clear in the process of learning is that until the light turns on, you may find yourself in the dark. With mindful practice we can see how we move from novice to expert to novice again, constantly – just like the transition from junior school to high school, when we move from being the oldest and most knowledgeable, ruling the school yard and towering above the younger children, to once again being the smallest, earnestly needing to recalibrate to a whole new system. This ebb and flow can be a wonderfully humbling experience if we surrender to it. Learning to be self-aware and accepting of what you don't know, can help you identify where to go next. No matter how in the dark you feel when you learn, there is always a path to the light.

The Courage
to Learn

Self-efficacy is the belief in our own abilities to meet challenges and successfully complete tasks. It is the kind of belief that can fill our sails with enough wind to propel us through our learning journey, and protect ourselves from feedback that might otherwise leave us feeling like a vessel full of holes. For some, a strong confidence in learning seems to come naturally. But not all of us have a shining perception of our ability as students. A lack of efficacy can be the anchor that drags us down, preventing us from moving forwards. Without the confidence to learn, we might even keep ourselves safely docked in the bay, checked out of learning entirely before we even start.

So how can mindfulness help us fortify our self-efficacy and give us the courage to learn?

LETTING GO

Our self-efficacy is shaped by the events of our past and influences our ideas of the future. With the practice of mindfulness, we can let go of the past. Our preconceived ideas about how good we are (or aren't) don't serve us when they are built on experiences that we consider to be failures. A loss or failure is not a strike against our character or ability.

If anyone has ever watched a baby or small child, it is clearly evident that the process of learning to walk involves a lot of falling down. Recognizing this as an inherent part of learning will equip you with the resilience necessary for success. Self-efficacy is what gives us the courage to fall, because we know that winning is not the be-all and end-all. When I was very young, my father printed and laminated a poem for me by Norman Vincent Peele, part of which captured the importance of self-belief: 'Life's battles don't always go to the stronger or faster man. But sooner or later, the man who wins is the man who thinks he can.'

SAVOUR SUCCESS

The belief that you can succeed is built from the experiences where you did succeed, so recognizing your successes is a vital way to build your self-efficacy. Mindfulness can help us not only pause to celebrate our successes, but also to savour them. So often in our journey of learning, our sights are always set on the distance, looking ahead to the next assignment, the next test, the next semester. But when we cultivate living in the present moment through a practice of mindfulness, we give ourselves the opportunity to relish the moments of achieving.

Savouring your achievements is beyond recognizing them. It is *feeling* them. When we achieve something, we might feel powerful, elated, excited, surprised or thrilled. If we don't slow down enough to notice these significant moments in our journey of life and study, they can lose their impact and the reward is watered down, drowned out by the lists of tasks that are still waiting to be done. Frame your degree or diplomas and put them on the wall. Take yourself out to lunch when you finish an assignment and toast yourself for a job well done. Tick off your lists as you get through them, and set aside time to notice and dwell on the times you meet your goals, no matter how small they are. Cultivate the verbal reinforcement of your capabilities by surrounding yourself with people whom you admire and who speak positively about you and themselves.

THE FIRST STEP

Don't make judgements on your capacity to learn just because there are things you don't know or can't do. Not knowing is simply an opportunity to learn something you have not yet mastered. I like to remind my students, when they say 'I can't do this', to rephrase with 'I can't do this yet'. Acknowledging or discovering what we don't know now or can't yet do is the first step to mastery. All you need is the self-belief that you can do what needs to be done, as long as you try hard enough.

Being smart is not a thing we are or are not, but is developed and acquired over time. It is estimated that our brain has around 100 billion neurons – around the same number of stars as there are in the Milky Way galaxy. Each neuron can form thousands of links, and these synaptic pathways are being made and pruned constantly. Your brain's ability to learn can be trained and cultivated, like any muscle. This very simple awareness can be a powerful beacon to return to, whenever you need reminding that your capacity to learn is probably far greater than you give yourself credit for.

Learning
to Learn

Socrates famously said, 'To know yourself is the beginning of wisdom.' Self-knowledge is powerful to us as students. There may be no better way to increase your success in your studies than by learning to understand your unique study preferences. As you move towards a deeper knowledge of yourself through mindfulness, you have the capacity to figure out the methods and techniques of scholarship that fit uniquely with you.

Educational theories have suggested that we all learn in different ways. Every brain is wired differently. Some of us gravitate towards images, preferring to see ideas mapped visually, or remembering information better when we draw or illustrate it. Some of us might recall things best when we create songs and ditties, or are most engaged when we read or write ideas. Many of us need to engage with our hands and bodies, learning kinaesthetically. Some of us learn best in groups, where we can talk through ideas and connect with people; others prefer to work solo.

As mindful learners we can tune into an awareness of how we learn, and which conditions of learning we uniquely thrive in. We have all noticed times where learning just clicks for us, but have we carefully observed the conditions of these instances and the nuances of our responses? If we sensitively observe ourselves while trying a variety of learning approaches, we can identify the ways of learning that really work for us. You will feel it when your attention snaps into vibrant clarity or when a jolt of enthusiasm energizes you. Take note of such moments. Such insights can inform the methods we use to study.

Conversely, there is also a wealth of self-knowledge to be found when we are particularly challenged by a way of learning. When you find that something is not working for you, do you disconnect or do you take this opportunity to move even closer to that experience and learn from it? The times you might want to skip an activity can be highly insightful. Perhaps you feel reluctant to do group work, or hate the idea of having to read a book? What you are not interested in or avoidant of can reveal areas that you can grow from, or cultivate your skills in. Just as we move towards those practices that we connect with, we can also be conscious not to avoid practices just because they are hard for us. Perhaps you can find creative ways to enrich these experiences. For instance, if you find reading alone unrewarding, try reading to someone and share and discuss the text together.

PLAY & CREATIVITY

There is no better way to discover new learning styles and approaches than through being playful with study. When we engage our creativity, we can transform knowledge in multiple ways. Write or talk about it, draw it, sing it; group knowledge together in unexpected ways. Discover what makes things interesting for you, and make this discovery an essential part of your learning. What we sprinkle on top of our bread-and-butter learning experience is what gives it its spice and flavour. Even if your teachers do the basics, when you get home, revise with all the imagination, colour and creativity you can think of until you find what you naturally respond to and what makes the experience something you want to continue.

Transforming knowledge into something personal, unique and fun is what really fires our brains. Through observing ourselves while we study we will come to know what the carrots are that will keep us going on our learning journey. Stagnating at your desk is not going to convince your brain to play ball. It will most likely put you straight to sleep and certainly won't keep you coming back for more. When you approach study in a style that really suits you, it's possible to bring a playfulness to your tasks. Learning doesn't have to be dry or serious to be effective. Quite the opposite, actually. There is no set way that we must learn, so use your study as a means to mindfully discover how you learn, and in doing so, find new ways to teach yourself.

Learning is an art. To master this art is to discover and invent the unique style in which you learn best. Finding combinations of techniques, methods and conditions for study that work for you is part of the joy of your journey as a life-long learner. It is also a route to deeper self-understanding. If your brain is an instrument, why not learn how it works and how to play it like a master?

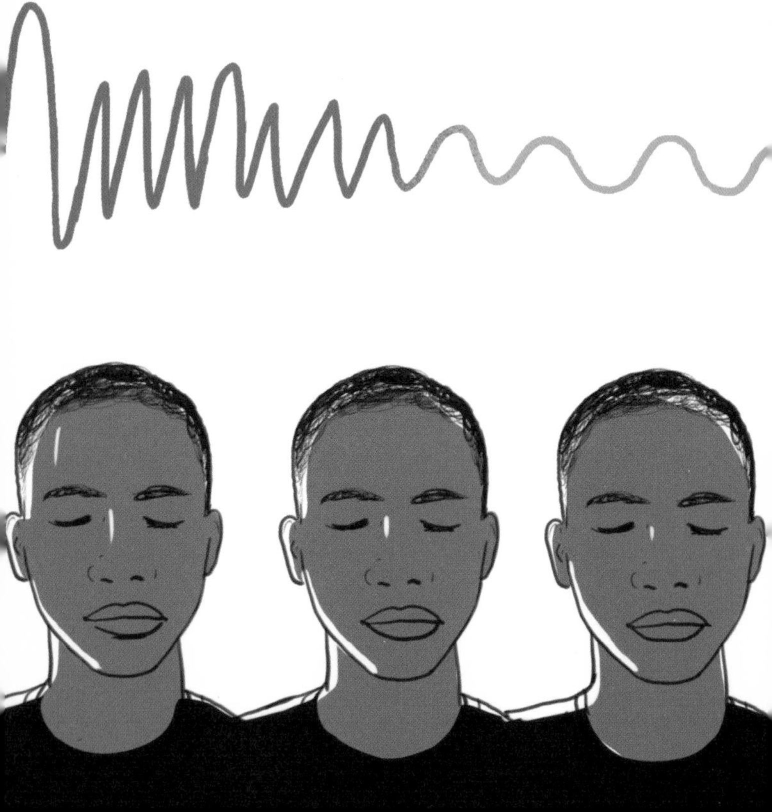

Transcending
Stress

Learning can be fun and rewarding but let's face it, it can also be incredibly stressful. We probably have all experienced times of high stress in our studies. Whether we haven't left enough time to prepare or perhaps there has just been too much on our plate and not enough time to get it all done, the stress associated with high pressure can be overwhelming.

At such times we might try to work frenetically through the stress and press on until the crescendo of anxiety passes with time or leaves us an absolute mess. Periods of acute stress can leave us paralysed with fear and unable to think, let alone study or perform well. Such things are not good for our health. Not surprisingly, research also tells us that when we reduce stress we have clearer thoughts. So how do we clear the skies of a stressed-out mind?

A LITTLE, NOT A LOT

The Chinese word for stress is made up of two characters: 'strong' and 'pressure'. This elegantly formed term for the concept refers to the conditions of stress, not our response to it or its effect. The term stress has negative connotations, associated with the detrimental impacts that prolonged acute pressure can have on us; however, stress – a state of being under strong pressure – is only negative when it squeezes us to the point of breaking.

There are some significant benefits to mild stress in study. In times of stress, our heart rate increases, our adrenaline spikes, our mind focuses and our breath quickens. While we generally dislike the nerves we feel before giving a speech, it is often this heightening of the nervous system that helps us perform.

However, stress is not a condition we are meant to experience for extended lengths of time. Short bursts of high performance require us to regulate back to homeostasis, our deferred calm state of being. But for many of us as students, the stress response lingers too long, and often escalates.

TUNE IN & BREATHE OUT

Mindfulness has been proven to reduce stress by acting like a circuit breaker, reducing activity in the part of the brain that is central to switching on our stress response – the amygdala. If we are mindful, we can become aware of our stress response and our unique patterns of behaviour. Stress doesn't have just a single flavour. It can be felt in a myriad of complex ways with various levels. Having a mindful attitude to your stress is about approaching it with curiosity, acceptance and non-judgement. Tuning into your body and identifying the stress signals in an accepting and compassionate way can help you respond with greater wisdom.

Quite often, stress manifests in the body very subtly in its fledgling state. Sensitive awareness of your body can bring you back to earth with more ease than you might think. Try moving towards the physical expressions of your stress. Notice where you feel the stress creeping into your body. Observe your heart rate. Is your breath shallow or quick? Note the locale of your physical tension – is it forming in your neck, your jaw, shoulders or back? As you take in more of the experience, stress diminishes. Through the regular practice of observing your body, you can take a step back and pick up on the stress signals that your body is communicating.

When you notice subtle signs of stress, it's time to take a break. Try practising 5 minutes of deep breathing. Lie down, focus on your body and feel the rise and fall of your chest as your lungs expand, returning to your breath every time you notice your mind wandering. Notice any change in your breath after giving yourself that time. You might also go for a walk, stretch your body or talk to someone about how you are feeling. An early awareness of stress may give you time to renegotiate your timeframe or reduce the amount of things you have on that week.

LIFE LESSONS

No matter how much pressure you might be under, making time to tune into your body, emotions and thoughts is critical. Don't put it off or think you are too busy. It is often during the high-pressure times when you feel you don't have the time to be mindful that it is most important to stop what you are doing and observe yourself. Having a consistent practice of mindfulness can support you during the high-pressure times. Repeated practice builds familiarity and can lead to something of a default mode of self-observation in times of pressure. The rhythmic quality to study, which repeatedly circles back to exams and the end-of-semester crunch time, allows these periods of high pressure to become anticipated opportunities to practise mindfulness, and a perfect training ground for your life and future stress.

Habit, Routine &
Ritual

A routine, done often enough, will become a habit. When something becomes a habit, it is often done automatically, without conscious thought, and we find that our mind starts to drift elsewhere. But when we are mindful of our habits, and conscious during our routines, we bring awareness and intentional focus to certain parts of our day, and this can have a wonderfully anchoring quality for us in our daily lives as students.

Each morning before starting study, I take a long, warm shower. I feel the water and the warmth on my body, soaking up the sounds and watching the water droplets on the glass. I give myself those moments to just *be*, trying not to think about yesterday or to anticipate what comes next or what is due. I practise being wholly present. So many of us rush the ordinary routines of our day or find our minds elsewhere. But when we absorb ourselves in the repeated activities that we do daily, such as the simple act of presently watching the warm steam rise as we shower, we can nourish and settle the mind, body and spirit.

Such routines can help create a quiet mental space to gently transition from one part of our day into another and ready the mind for study. Building in a mindful prelude to your study can be a powerful way to start work. No matter what routine you establish for yourself, be it a shower taken slowly and intentionally, a short walk, 5 minutes of slow breathing, or dancing around to an uplifting song, preparing yourself for study with mindful presence can help you shake off any lingering moods that threaten to sidetrack you and set the tone for a productive day.

THE MAGIC OF RITUALS

Just as our routines over time become habits, so too can our habits become rituals, if they are done mindfully and solemnly, with a sense of reverence and slowness. Daily rituals are like the cool, smooth stepping-stones that we rest on as we navigate through our busy days – micro-events of magic that we look forward to, which create a sense of calm and grounding to our days and weeks.

We can make ritual out of any mundane task if it is done with a mindset to make it special. All we need do is bring our present awareness to our actions, ourselves and the space and objects around us, and pay attention as though we are savouring a rare delight. This might be catching the sunshine on your yoga mat for a few stretches to tune into yourself. Or making a chai and taking it outside to drink, inhaling its spiced scent, feeling the warmth of it emanating to your hands from the ceramic cup, sipping it slowly as you watch the breeze dancing and swaying through the trees. By breaking up a day of study with such practices, our moments of mindfulness can become something we look forward to and work towards, moments that nurture us and soothe our souls.

MINDFULNESS AS A HABIT

The phrase 'a force of habit' refers to the inherent momentum that a habit has. A regular routine pulls us into its familiarity, building a weight of its own over time. The routines we set and keep for ourselves eventually become automatic habits, and that includes intentional planned practices of mindfulness. Study particularly lends itself to routines and is therefore a perfect time to establish a habit of mindfulness. When we are part of an educational institution, our study schedules often come with in-built structure, allowing us to slot small mindful practices into the routines of student life. Perhaps you might get to class 5 minutes early for a little mindful colouring to cultivate stillness, or walk slowly barefoot across the courtyard to feel the grass beneath your feet before meeting your study group at the café. Associating mindful practices with certain times of day or activities can help you build the habit into your study.

We will naturally create for ourselves habits and routines. But with the self-awareness that comes with mindfulness, we can be more intentional about the way we form our habits and routines, to better support us in our scholarly practices, and nourish us along the way. The routines that are already there in our day can become powerfully calming if we use them to still our minds and be fully present. These moments can be the pauses that punctuate the daily grind and create little windows for us to look within ourselves.

Self-care & Your
Physical Self

Self-care might feel like a luxury you don't have time for as a student. In the busyness of student life, it is all too easy to end up eating 2-minute noodles, hydrating with coffee and getting very little sleep, particularly in high-pressure periods. Engrossed in an assignment or project, we can lose ourselves in a state of flow and emerge hours later, ravenous and exhausted.

A great deal of the nature of study happens in the brain. But being in the head so much can lead to a strong disconnect with the body, and neglect of our physical needs. What we eat and drink and how we use our bodies has a huge impact on the outcomes of our studious efforts. Quality food, regular hydration and oxygen is all essential fuel for the brain. Ultimately, the sustainability of our studies depends on our ability to know how to take care of ourselves.

LISTEN IN & RESPOND

You don't need to read up on the science of best study diets to know what your body needs. All you need to do is observe your body mindfully and respond in turn. The body is communicating all the time if you learn how to listen. As a young student, I used to study with a bowl of lollies and other 'encouragement' food, totally unaware that after the initial high from the sugar, I would then find myself flagging with the subsequent hypoglycaemic low. I failed to feel the correlation between the food and the mood, or perhaps I felt it, but didn't notice it. Sensation, when not intentionally observed, can be like something seen on the periphery of our vision; it is there, but not so clear that we recognize it consciously in our mind.

In a practice of mindfulness we can choose a primary object of attention on which to focus. As a student, choosing the body as the object of our focus allows us to listen in to the physical experience of study. This might be the feeling of tired dry eyes, an ache in the lower back from sitting for too long, or the grumble of a hungry belly. It could be observing tiredness or a cloudy mind, or a brain full of energy and clarity. In choosing the physical experience as our object of focus, we can continually bring ourselves back to witness ourselves in the act of learning.

This embodied awareness of your physical self is a way to collect a wealth of information with which to wisely respond to the constantly changing needs of your body. Listen for the body's inbuilt alarm system, pain, which becomes a strong cue to stop what you are doing. If you observe tense muscles, pause and respond with some neck stretches and shoulder rolls, or take a walk; moving your muscles oxygenates the brain and can improve focus, as well as shaking off tensions in your body. If your brain is cloudy, try sitting and meditating, focusing on your breath in and out. Investing in these little moments of mindfulness can yield great returns.

AN INTENTION FOR SELF-CARE

Much of caring for ourselves is common sense: drinking enough water, eating fresh and varied food, taking regular exercise and getting plenty of sleep are all simple things that will stand us in good stead. But we often put off this essential self-care, deferring the fundamental needs of our bodies to what can seem like more pressing deadlines. When we ignore these needs, we accrue a debt that will eventually come due. But, when we set the intention to have a gentle, mindful practice of study, the signals of our body become something we choose to respond to with compassionate self-care.

There are mornings where I feel less able to write, with my mind dull and sleepy, my body slow and tired. At times like this, I let go of being productive for a moment and lean in to myself, listening closely to how

I am feeling and responding in turn. If you are in tune with your body and mind, you too can appreciate when it becomes futile pushing on, when it's time to switch your intention from productivity to self-care.

A strong mind-body connection, fostered by a habit of mindfulness, will greater serve your goals in the long run. It's all about finding a balance. When you take care of your essential needs, you will have more to give to your study. Your body is the extraordinary vessel that carries you through your study journey. If you look after it with love and compassion, you will last the distance to discover that life and scholarship isn't a sprint – it's a marathon.

Finding Your
Off Switch

After a full day, and sometimes night, of study, we
fall fatigued into our beds, ready to slip into the soft,
velvet embrace of sleep. Yet how often, even in our
exhaustion, is our brain still whirring frenetically like
a wind-up toy, preventing our rest and holding us
captive in a mental state of activity rather than rest.
If our brains are blackboards overflowing with
information, where do we find the duster?

We know how vital it is to be well-rested in order to
concentrate and take in all the new knowledge of a
day's learning. Countless studies tell us that a good
night's sleep is crucial to performing well in exams.
Yet, no matter how much we want to rest, sometimes

sleep evades us, like an elusive sprite that we can't quite manage to grasp. At such times, shifting into a state of mindfulness can ease our overworked minds back into a state of calm. A simple practice of mindfulness can be the circuit breaker needed to reboot our brain to a lower frequency, slowing down the deluge of information that threatens to overwhelm us, and replacing it with a sense of calm. Quieting the brain through mindful techniques is a powerful yet simple tool that is essential for every student's arsenal.

MAKING THE SWITCH

The old remedy for sleeplessness, counting sheep, is based on the idea of setting the mind on a single object or point of focus. This is actually a technique of mindful practice. However, rather than making imaginary sheep your object of attention, try taking note of your body. While it may be obvious that your mind is hyped up, you might find that this tension is also reflected in your body. Before you get into bed, lie down on a yoga mat or carpet and take a mental inventory of your body from head to toe, calmly observing every muscle. Doing this wind-down before you get into bed prepares your body for sleep and prevents the frustration of feeling you have been in bed for ages without drifting off.

Hitting your off switch is about calming your nervous system and winding the body and mind down from performance (or stress) mode to rest mode. When I lie down in bed at night, I can hear my parasympathetic nervous system (the 'rest and digest' system) switch on, because my stomach starts to gently gurgle. Some days it takes longer to get there than others. It might require a number of different mindful approaches, or objects of focus. Perhaps these objects of attention might be feeling the soft bed and cushioned embrace of linen under the body. Sometimes I turn on my diffuser with some essential oils and engage my olfactory sense. The attention can then shift to the breath. Mentally note your body's natural breathing rhythm while you internally think 'in' as you inhale and 'out' as you exhale.

You might note the temperature of the air as it passes through your nostrils, cool in and warm out. In the quiet of night, when everything is so still, it can be possible to feel more sensitively the beat of the heart in the body. Slowly scan your whole body to note where you can feel your pulse – sometimes in the chest, other times in the stomach, or the arms.

JUST BEING

Most importantly, as you embody the physical moment, try not to judge or scold yourself for not sleeping. Having compassion for your body and mind, which have worked so hard for you over the day, can help bring your evening to a close with a mindset of gratitude, rather than self-criticism. Of course it is hard to be tired and unable to sleep, but these moments of sleeplessness, like all moments, will eventually pass and you will soon enough slip into sleep. How gracefully you can accept these moments – moving deeply into the experience of them, rather than anticipating what is next or what is to come tomorrow – can determine how quickly you finally arrive at your desired destination.

If it is your busy mind that is keeping you up, be a passive listener to its stories. Perhaps it has a path of its own to walk, recounting and wandering in aimless fashion as it winds down. Breathe deeply and quietly listen in to yourself. When we observe the brain in its jitterbug moments and withhold comment, stepping back from engagement and allowing it to run its course, we can surrender to our current state and reduce the potential of worsening the situation. Rather than actively trying to go to sleep, hold yourself in the present, until you organically drift off into the sweet dreams that await.

Avoiding
Burnout

As a new day dawns, we rise again to another day of learning. Some days we wake up full of vim and vigour, while others we are not in the mood at all. We might feel a little creaky, our mental cogs reluctant to move. Such feelings of sluggishness aren't just limited to mornings either. Let's face it, as students we can experience a fair amount of apathy, laziness and lack of enthusiasm for our study at any time of day. So what do we do when we find ourselves in a place of tiredness?

We can warm up a congealed state of mind with the energy of mindful observation and inward attention. If you find you are slow to start when you sit down to study, make your fatigue the object of your attention.

Notice where you feel it. Is it centred in your mind or your body? Taking some time to walk outside can help the blood to start flowing and give you an opportunity to take stock, checking in with the sensations and feelings in your mind and body.

DECIPHERING FATIGUE

Sometimes when we are tired, rest is best. It is important when we identify fatigue to exercise self-compassion and self-care. However, there are also plenty of times where we really don't need the additional sleep. Being able to observe feelings of fatigue from a mindful perspective can help us to recognize when we really need rest, and when there is something else happening. Such self-knowledge allows us the wisdom to make the distinction between self-compassion and self-hindrance when it comes to stopping or avoiding work.

Feeling too tired or unmotivated for your study might indicate there is something you need to look at.

This is not to encourage over-analysis; rather, you should hold this notion lightly and take a look at what is present. Perhaps your apathy for a class after lunch is less about a midday slump and more about your feelings about a teacher or a shaken confidence in a subject. As mindful students we become aware of the signals of inertia to help us discover the root of it.

Tiredness can also be an appropriate regulator to how much and how quickly we are able to process new learning, slowing down the intake of information to a level that we are able to work through. In my first degree I used to wade my way through readings which I could barely comprehend. There was a levelling up in this process of reading, trying to piece together information that I could understand with that of the subject-specific language that was entirely foreign to me at the time. Inevitably after a long session of reading, I would be overwhelmed with tiredness and fall asleep.

OBSERVE, DON'T INDULGE

Our thoughts can trigger emotions and moods, just as they can prolong and sustain them. Giving unwise attention to mental states can hinder us greatly in our study. Indulging in thoughts like 'I am really tired' and 'I can't be bothered' can reinforce and hold us in that state of being. As you bear witness to your experience of fatigue, try to simply mentally note your feelings and thoughts. This can be done with impartial curiosity, without judgement or building a narrative around your experience. Observe the tone of the voice in your mind as you mentally note sensations and feelings. Is it impartial, or does it sound more like a whinge or complaint? This can provide important feedback.

TURN UP UNTIL THE MAGIC HAPPENS

Periods of tiredness and torpidity, like all states, are temporary. Regardless of how ready you feel to learn, mindfulness teaches us that whatever you might be feeling at this moment, will pass. The wonderful characteristic of mindfulness is learning to be with all the states as they arise and to stay present, accompanying them until they pass. So if you wake up and find yourself sleepy, turn up to your work and be with that state as you gently do what you can. We need not indulge in the state of tiredness for it to go away.

The most important thing we need to do as students is turn up. Part of the challenge of entering into any activity is to start it, and this is certainly the case with study. We have to open the book, sit at the desk, be in the class. Even if we aren't feeling the enthusiasm, turning up and doing our best to tune in is the only way to get our study done. Even if we think nothing is happening, if we keep persevering, simply being present as we go through the motions, our efforts will eventually bear fruit.

Study
Space

Cultivating and keeping an inviting study space can prepare us for productive and pleasurable study sessions and keep them happening. Through mindfulness we can develop a sense of awareness of our surroundings and the effect they have on us. The Eastern art of Feng Shui recognizes that our living spaces are fundamental to the wellbeing and success of our lives. However, we don't need to become experts in this ancient tradition to make the most of the reciprocity between our study space and our success. We need only develop awareness of our lived experience of our working environments by paying attention to our emotions and physical states while we are in our space of study and respond in turn.

FEEDBACK & RESPONSE

Observe yourself when you walk into your study space. Our thoughts and feelings provide vital feedback on our surroundings. Is it a place where you like to be? Is it inviting, calming or inspiring? Perhaps you feel overwhelmed when you enter your study? Or maybe you find you get tired quickly or easily distracted? Once we form an awareness between ourself and our environment we can adapt and modify our surroundings for greater affect.

If you find yourself distracted, remove the things that are catching and diverting your attention. Be honest with yourself. If an object isn't serving your purpose, move it elsewhere. If you feel overwhelmed walking into your study space, perhaps there are too many things in it. If you notice you tire quickly, maybe you need more fresh air or natural sunlight in your workspace. If there is no window, consider bringing greenery into your study space with an indoor plant. Be discerning in the way you curate your environment and be willing to shape it specifically and intentionally for your needs as you notice them.

There is no one perfect design for a study space that sets us up for success, because we are all so individual. Being surrounded by lots of books and pictures might be inspiring for some, distracting for others. Only by observing ourselves and the way we respond to our space, and being intentional about the way we shape it, can we develop a study environment uniquely suited to ourselves.

CHANGING SPACES

You might find, like me, you prefer multiple environments to work in and respond well to variety in your workplace. I enjoy different study spaces for different purposes and am rarely in my home study. For instance, when reading and taking notes I love to be in a big library or lying in a park under a tree, but when writing an assignment, I prefer to be in a hub of activity, like a café. In one instance I need stillness and silence, while in the other I work better with a low and constant hum of noise and activity. Studying can be isolating and lonely at times, so it can be helpful to move your workspace outside to feel part of the world.

CLEAN SPACE, CLEAR MIND

As quickly as we might find a space that works for us, it may also change. With each new project or at the end of a study cycle, I like to refresh my space. Changing and rearranging our study space can invigorate us and reset our frame of mind, a little like defragmenting a computer. As we sort through all the things on our desk, reordering, filing or throwing away, we make space for our mind to do the same thing.

It is no coincidence that our physical and mental spaces reflect and affect each other. In the practice of yoga, saucha – a niyama: one of the eight limbs of yoga – encourages a personal practice of cleanliness. It is based on the premise that a consistent practice of cleaning and clearing encourages a clear mind, stillness in one's emotions and clarity of thought. As we clean, arrange and tidy our study space, we can use this opportunity to observe our thoughts and feelings. While we sweep away mess and put everything in its place, the mind too can quietly reorder, find calm and settle. Tidying our space before we begin to study can be an opportunity not only to clear the mind and make our space inviting, but also to set intentions and gather enthusiasm for our work.

The spaces that we study and work in have an impact on us. They can also tell us a lot about how we are feeling. When we see our study environments as an extension of ourselves and cultivate awareness of how we interact with them, we empower ourselves with greater self-knowledge and the capacity to respond wisely in turn.

Teamwork
& Tea Breaks

Study can be lonely and tough to do on your own. Being part of a team can make the student journey far more productive, and more enjoyable too – some of our best lifelong friendships can be forged under the pressures of study. In the sharing of resources, knowledge and support, in teamwork and tea breaks, we can find a certain buoyancy to weather the challenges of study.

But the social aspect of learning can yield much conflict and social angst too. Among our learning communities can be found great diversity, passion, strong opinions and conflicting values and views. When we are knitted together with others in the context of our schools and universities, the wise communication and community-building that mindfulness can bring helps to greatly enrich and foster positive outcomes to our teamwork and our learning.

Teachers love to put students together in groups for assessment, and with good cause. If we can learn to work well together in class, we can apply this later to our lives and livelihoods – hopefully. But it can be with a certain amount of trepidation that we respond to a teacher's declaration that the next assessment will be a group task. Being thrown into a collective of people whom we may not know or even like, let alone work well with, can have quite a negative effect on our grades and on each other. When gathering in groups, there is always a possibility that there will be personality clashes, conflict, disagreement and perhaps an uneven distribution of the workload. So how can mindfulness help?

MINDFUL LISTENING

One of the fundamental skills to working well with others is mindful listening – being fully present and focused in your attention when another is speaking. Listening mindfully goes beyond polite etiquette. It is not simply waiting for your turn to talk, or actively nodding and making eye contact. When you mindfully listen, you direct attention away from your natural inclination to mentally respond. You cease preparing for your opportunity to speak next, and instead pause your thoughts to move deeply into the present moment.

The person speaking becomes the object of attention. Your focus may be not just on what they are saying, but the way they say it. Witness their body language, the tone and the pauses of their delivery. Observe the way they breathe, their facial expressions, where they look. Using all of your senses, absorb their communication. The respect that we offer each other as mindful listeners cultivates a sense of safety for those who are sharing and validates their effort through our sincere concentration.

RESPECT & OBJECTIVITY

Mindful listening also comes from a place of fostering humility. It requires us to accept that others may have something to teach us that we don't already know. As mindful learners in a group, we can become more inquisitive, open to discover and learn from one another. As we observe those around us, it is important to refrain from passing judgement. Passively observe yourself as you start to form ideas about what a person is saying and let the thoughts pass. Hold off from any deep analysis too. Because as soon as we start to form judgement, appraisal or response, we slip away from the present moment and shift our focus back to internalized rhetoric. Essentially, as soon as we start judging and mentally responding, we stop listening.

If you are occupied with mindful listening in your group, when it comes to your opportunity to speak, you can do so with greater authenticity. Rather than having a pre-anticipated speech ready in mind, you must draw your response from your mind in the moment, slowly and with full consideration of all that has been shared. You might surprise yourself to find that the view you started with has been enriched by the ideas of others, or even changed entirely.

PART OF A WHOLE

Bearing close and objective witness to people within our collective of study naturally builds compassion and care. We might see the nerves of our peers, or sense the lack of confidence another might have. If we can notice these things, we can offer our encouragement or support. As we see others and their ideas more clearly, we can cultivate an awareness of ourselves as just one part of a wider community. This enables us to realize we can never see the entire picture of our learning from where we stand, on our own. As mindful students, we move to the comprehension that when we learn together and share, we build a greater collective knowledge through each of our unique perspectives.

Connecting
with our Teachers

Mindfulness can positively affect our relationships and enrich the way we communicate when approached with authenticity, intention and self-awareness. Through mindful communication, we can foster authentic relationships with those who teach us, and make the most of the opportunities to learn from them.

The old hierarchical notion of all-knowing teachers imparting their knowledge to quiet, submissive learners is outdated, and rightly so. Knowledge is a vast reservoir, and it is impossible for a teacher to know everything! Today, students are expected to be proactive and able to seek out their own knowledge, full of questions, reflections and higher-order thinking. This go-getter attitude is not something that can be achieved if we are passive learners with a belief that the teacher before us already has all the answers. Approaching learning with curiosity and confidence requires us to see ourselves as worthy peers on a learning journey with our teachers.

Shaking off a passive learning attitude requires a shift in consciousness. Here, mindfulness helps us to introspectively observe our thinking and patterns of behaviour. For instance, if you want to know something, do you first seek the answer yourself or do you ask your teacher? If your teacher gives you an answer do you always accept it as gospel or do you fact-check? When you regularly check in with yourself, it becomes easier and quicker to identify when you are slipping into laziness, waiting for knowledge to be imparted rather than stepping into your power as a learner.

BUILDING RELATIONSHIPS

Relationships can be so much about reciprocity; what we give we often get back. An exciting teacher who it feels good to be in the classroom with is more inspirational. The development of positive relationships with our teachers can be greatly helped through a practice of mindfulness. When we are mindful, we gain a greater understanding of what is happening around us, as well as what is happening inside us. This attentiveness to the here and now extends to those around us. Through mindfulness we can learn to see beyond ourselves and our own needs, extending our attention and awareness to how our choices can affect and influence others.

As students we have the ability to set some of the tone of our relationships by the intentions we communicate when we interact with our teachers. Being in the present moment and developing your ability to sustain focus shows consideration to your teacher, and can greatly improve the way they feel about you in their classroom. When you are in a class or lecture, be there wholeheartedly; commit yourself to that moment of learning, consciously and with intention. How serious we are about our learning is something that is inherently communicated to our teachers through our actions.

When you first walk into a classroom, where do you choose to sit? Be mindful how sitting front and centre will communicate something different to picking a seat up the back corner. Do you turn up to class on time? Are you early, or forever rushing in late? We often think of ourselves from our perspective as an individual, but in the context of a classroom environment, we are one part of a whole. Like a drop of water in a lake, our actions will ripple outwards and impact on others. Observe how being late to class affects the teacher and the rest of the students, unsettling attention and perhaps even changing the mood. When we notice the waves that follow our actions, through the simple practice of noticing, we can grow as individuals and choose more considerate behaviours that foster a more positive learning environment for all of us.

AUTHENTIC ENQUIRY

Communicating with our teachers with courage and authenticity helps us build relationships with them that are based on trust, honesty and openness. Be willing to question your teachers and even (respectfully) challenge them if you disagree. If you don't understand something, speak up and ask for help. If you didn't complete an assignment, don't make excuses, take a deep breath and tell your teacher why. If you are stressed, let them know. No one can offer you help if you aren't showing your hand. Move towards authenticity with your teachers and see what happens.

When we are mindful, we automatically move towards communicating more authentically and living more intentionally. By interacting with sincerity and openness with our teachers, it opens up space for our teachers to mirror this authenticity, and we can move towards meaningful and empowering learning experiences, full of curiosity and energy.

Navigating the
Virtual Terrain

Online learning is a relatively new platform in education, giving us all access to study in a way that previously wasn't always possible. But this academic interface can be a lonely one. When we learn remotely we can feel disconnected from many of the vital experiences we would usually have as students. For many of us, this new territory presents ways of interacting that feel very unfamiliar, at times exhausting and even demotivating. Mindfulness can help us find our way through the discomforts that technology can bring, towards a more meaningful and enjoyable experience.

COMMUNITY & CONNECTION

There is something special about being on campus. Feeling part of a community and walking through the hallowed halls of an educational institution, you can't help but feel deeply connected to a culture of learning. But, in the absence of a school environment, it is possible for us to feel a strong disconnect. Being online means there are no incidental chats at the library or impromptu coffee catch-ups with your classmates after a lecture. The loss of this organic atmosphere and shared experience is one that we can mindfully acknowledge and it is totally natural to find ourselves feeling a little sad about it.

The casual, in-person encounters that happen in school allow us to discuss ideas or to raise our questions about a subject, as well as chatting about life outside of school. It is really important for our mental health that we have opportunities to talk with people who understand what we are experiencing. As an online learner, we can still seek these opportunities, it will just be in a different way.

Set the intention to foster a learning community among your peers and remain open and present for any opportunities as they arise. Put a Post-it note with the word 'Connect' on your computer to keep your mind attuned to this intention. Look for and join an online study group, discussion forums, or spark up friendships with fellow students via email. If you find no one has organized any groups, then why not step up and create them? Don't allow yourself to give up on community and connection if this feels like something you need or enjoy about study. If you observe the need for it within yourself, it's likely others are feeling that way too.

THE NEW NORMAL

Part of the discomfort we may experience in virtual learning environments can be caused by attempting to apply the same social norms for in-person interactions, to a totally different interface. Eye contact and body language is a key way we communicate, but online lectures mean we lose ourselves in the crowd. Lagging connections and the absence of non-verbal cues can give us a cognitive overload as we try to make sense of everything. Recognizing that online learning brings with it a steep learning curve can help us be kind to ourselves. Allow yourself space to feel and experience the online environment without having to pretend it is comfortable.

After online lectures, try taking a few minutes to sit quietly with eyes closed, focusing on the breath. Through this mindful practice we can make a little more sense of this realm where our minds are together but our bodies are not. Turn off your camera, mute your sound and have a lie down when you can. Move around and stretch. Go outside and get some fresh air. Communicate with your lecturers and let them know what is challenging you. Give yourself permission to try and find a work-around, rather than just suffering and accepting.

Keeping yourself motivated can be a challenge, but a change of scenery can be key to keeping you feeling enlivened. Try working from your local café sometimes, or even relocating to a different room can be energising.

Having some time away from working at home can also allow you an opportunity to be completely unavailable to those you live with. Studying from home can make you far too accessible and amplifies guilt that you should be involved in the family, or doing chores. Tune into your need to set and maintain boundaries by communicating your work hours and availability and sticking to them.

WALKING A NEW PATH

Learning online is relatively new territory. Recognizing that you are in the midst of learning to exist in an entirely different social environment can help you approach your online learning experience with curiosity, reduced expectations and less judgement. Take the negative parts of your experience and start to see them as vital feedback. Mindfulness is characterized by a kind of surrender to the experience of life and a curious observation of this experience and your response to it. Through mindfulness you can be more present to take note of how you are feeling and respond in turn.

Connecting
with the Text

Have you ever found you have read a whole page and not taken in a single word? Your eyes can be sequentially scanning left to right on the page but mentally you are entirely somewhere else. Reading can be a large part of our work as students, and provides a quintessential opportunity to practise mindfulness: by intentionally choosing to read in a focused and attentive way, we can make the most of our reading time, and at the same time exercise our habit of attending to the here and now.

For many of us, reading is often a form of multitasking, with text messages and banners, traffic signs and billboards all taken in as we hustle through our daily lives at an alarming pace. But as we nestle down with a book or article, we can slow down, and cue an agitated mind to settle into a place of clarity and relaxation. Stilling the mind from its habitual thinking by being fully aware and attentive in the act of reading can bring some much-needed stillness and emotional balance to our study.

THE OBJECT

While much reading is done digitally these days, there is something special about the tactility of a book. The book itself, weighted, textured, requiring constant attention in our holding of it, becomes an anchor for our concentration and state of alertness. It repeatedly reminds us, with each whispered turn of the page, of the here and now, in the subtle friction of one page caressing another. Time is marked by a different kind of measure, that of the turning page, revealing to us an insight of our experience of reading, as it is happening. The rhythm of our reading pace reflects our engagement with the text, an echo of the undulations of our attention and enthusiasm. Here, the pace quickens, in a moment of fascination, there it slows, as we scrutinize or struggle with a concept or turn of phrase.

The art of savouring is something that the Japanese exemplify in their tea ceremony. Every aspect of the experience is taken in, slowly and with full awareness. Books are aesthetic objects. We hold them in our hands, feeling the weight of them, appreciate the cover, the thought that has gone into the creation of this object, having passed through many hands to finally arrive in yours.

SLOW DOWN & SOAK IN

When you slow down, you change the experience of reading. Being in the moment with the text, without rushing, is about surrendering and allowing the process to take as long as it takes. When we read slowly and deeply, with curiosity, we open up to a reading experience that is further-reaching and more discerning. We might stop from time to time to savour a particularly rich or resonant phrase, to ask questions about the content or consider how it relates to the wider world.

Reading with a dictionary beside us, pausing to look up an unfamiliar word here and there, can slow reading even further and enrich our experience. This kind of relished reading allows for uncharted voyages of discovery. A dictionary is a map that accompanies our voyage into reading, and is the first port of call to understanding new things. Making unplanned side excursions into these treasures of new vocabulary and new ideas can make reading a delight.

Keeping your mind from wandering as you are reading study materials can be a challenge. Our thoughts can drift on a current of associated ideas, as we find our eyes moving over the words but our brain somewhere else. This can make a chapter feel like an endless endurance test. Rather than pushing on, give space to your reading and allow yourself some processing time. If you keep reading, your mind is divided, trying to concentrate on what you are taking in, while also trying to process what you have just read. Absorption takes time. If we water a plant, it takes time for the liquid to seep through the soil, weaving its way through root systems. If you pour too much water in at once, it simply overflows. It is the same for our brains. Give a little space, perhaps make a cup of tea, pause between one part of the text and another, and this will help us absorb what we are reading.

As a mindful reader we can move towards words with a sense of curiosity, joy and wonder. Through words, an idea is transported from one mind to another. The author decodes an abstract thought, and makes it visible through their words. As we read, we take it up into our minds where it is changed again, having been filtered through the lens of our own knowledge, experience and understanding. The process of reading is a kind of magic.

Mindful
Writing

Clear and concise writing can be an elusive art to many of us. As a young student I used to write my assignments like a kind of verbal diarrhoea on the computer. I would open a document and go hell for leather, each time ending up typing 5,000 words when I only needed 500. It was time-consuming and exhausting, to say the least. It requires a certain clarity of mind to be able to communicate in words, succinctly and with intention. Like an archer who hits the bullseye each time, there is a certain amount of practice that accompanies the ability to craft elegant sentences without the flood of extraneous words. The method of free writing that I used to engage in as a young student has its purposes, but it is like shooting a hundred arrows in the hope one might accidentally hit the target.

Prior to computers, such a haphazard approach would have been less feasible. Finite ink and paper would have brought with them a certain need for economy of words. There is no backspace or cut-and-paste with a typewriter, as there is on the laptop. It is easy to imagine that writing would have come more slowly and purposefully, with greater consideration and more pauses. The activity of writing would have been more mindful, involving listening to thought, selecting it with intention and with great care, reiterated on the page, consciously and with singular focus. With no auto-correct, a dictionary would have been on hand for those words where the writer was uncertain of the spelling. Each time, writing would stop, the meaning of a word would be reinforced – a pause in the train of thought, creating mental space for creation and ideas to bubble up.

TRANSPORTED TO A SLOWER TIME

To write mindfully is to imagine yourself back in the time of quill and paper or retro typewriter, and to flout expediency in exchange for a slowed and conscious approach to our use of words. Compose a sentence. Stop and take a breath. Look at the sentence and consider what it actually says. Does it communicate clearly and accurately what you wanted to say? Consider the readability of the text. Change it if you need to before moving on with the next sentence or paragraph. Take the rush out of the writing.

Acknowledge that word count does not indicate progress. The measure of success might instead be the accuracy of communication and the shape and form of prose as gracefully and intentionally crafted as a sculpture made from a single stone. The measure of success might also be the experience of writing as something pleasurable. Revel in the variety and possibly of words and the potential they give for communication and for understanding.

THE AESTHETIC OF WRITING

There is an aesthetic quality to writing. We need not always be on our computer. You might perhaps change to pencil and paper for your draft. Feel the grip of your fingers around your pencil. Hear the scratch of the graphite on paper and feel the subtle friction of it against the surface. Perhaps write with a calligraphy pen, a process which requires a certain awareness and embodied presence, engaging visually with the ink and using it with a sense of control, watching it as it dwindles, observing its change in flow and re-inking before it runs dry. Even the clatter of striking your computer keys can produce a kind of musical rhythm which can bring with it a feeling of delight.

FREE WRITING

While mindful awareness in writing can be exemplified by the slow and considered use of language and the embodied physical experience of writing, there is also a place for the thundering, surrendering outpouring of free writing. There is nothing like taking the handbrake off and writing fast and free, letting your words flow without judgement or consideration or care for correct spelling or grammar, allowing for whatever is arising in your mind to spill onto the page without hesitation. This sort of writing can purge writers' block, energize us and help us find an elusive phrase or expression trapped inside. Free writing is authentic writing, which occupies the mind so well we simply cannot be diverted. After such a deluge you may find the mind stilled once again, ready to softly engage with slow and considered writing once more, until staleness ensues and you are once again ready to run.

Mindful writing is writing with intention. It is being present in the act of writing, embodying the physical experience and observing the mental experience. When we write mindfully, we use the practice of writing as the focus for our meditation, during which we witness ourselves in the creative act. What beauty such an experience of writing might bring to the author.

Life
Studies

We are all learning, all the time. The notion that we should be confined to a classroom or desk goes against our very nature, yet it's a reality we often can't avoid as students of institutionalized learning. Given that it is reasonable to assume that a large portion of your educational experience is going to happen at a desk inside a classroom, it is up to you to seek a better balance. If you open yourself up to engaging regularly with different learning environments and learning experiences, your study in the classroom can become more dynamic.

Teachers are often allocated 40-minute lessons in which to teach, lecturers a little longer. They have their lesson plans, learning objectives and allocated students, and in the allotted time, they hope to convey with a certain amount of success whatever it is they are required to teach. How dry that sounds! Yet the nature of learning can be far more unpredictable and far more exciting than the experience we get in a classroom. Of course, teachers can only work with what they have been given, so there is no point blaming them. But what we can do is acknowledge that when we are at the helm, in our own time, we do not need to emulate the conditions of learning that we experience in schools, colleges and universities. We don't need to set time limits on how long we explore a topic, or how quickly we should be able to take up knowledge. Learning can take time, sometimes years. It took Leonardo da Vinci 16 years to paint the *Mona Lisa*. Conversely, we might sometimes grasp something quickly, in a sudden flash of insight and clarity, so why linger, unless we are interested?

NATURAL BORN LEARNERS

As small children, we learn by exploring, doing, being outside, watching others and engaging with each opportunity with curiosity and spontaneity. We were led by sheer enthusiasm, necessity and a desire to know. Children learn as they live, in the moment, with little expectation. As we grow older and engage with formal learning in institutions, we can lose sight of this very natural way of learning, forgetting our inherent drive for discovery. But we can reinvigorate our study through mindfully seeking ways to reconnect with our very nature. The simple act of observing ourselves slipping into the learned behaviour of sitting still to study, in a static way, can be enough to shake us out of such habits. Ask yourself, could you be studying somewhere else? Of course there is a time when we need to hit the books or ground ourselves at the computer to write an assignment, but so often we could instead be getting out and engaging with the vibrant learning resource that is the world around us.

LEARNING FROM LIFE

Learning away from your desk, away from the confines of a room, can electrify you. It is the charge that we often need to ignite the curiosity, passion and possibility that can propel us on our path of scholarship. Museums and galleries, libraries, novels and podcasts, films, talking to people and watching nature can all bring unexpected insights. We can step out of theory and closer to practice when we move towards learning through living. It is an astrophysicist taking time to star-gaze up into the skies, an art student visiting the paint maker to learn how to grind their own pigment, a budding architect travelling to experience the wonder of buildings old and new around the world. By meandering off the path to explore a rabbit warren of knowledge, you can be led by your intuition and pleasure.

Such an authentic, intuitive approach to learning serves to build within us a sense of trust in ourselves as learners. It opens our eyes to the possibility of finding and firming up understanding in the everyday moments.

As we look to the world around us for answers, rather than waiting for them to be instilled into us in a classroom, we become students of life. Just as a falling apple is said to have led Isaac Newton to his discovery of gravity, a student with their mind switched on and ready to learn outside the classroom holds the potential for knowledge far beyond the confines of the prescribed curriculum.

This interplay between institutionalized learning and intuitive self-directed learning is the magic combination for knowledge. But we require a practice of present awareness and observation in the moment of the world around us if we are to notice and discover what lies in wait. Mindfulness optimizes the habit of this readiness to learn and generates an openness to receive. Instead of being in a mindset of anticipating and expecting what will happen, we are watching, listening, asking and being present, just like we were as young children.

Pressing
Pause

There are times when we need to switch off from study. Taking a holiday from learning, be it even a brief one, is an essential part of being a student. Without proper rest, fatigue can set in, and we miss out on other aspects of life that ensure our education is holistic and well-rounded. Sometimes the most productive thing we can do for our study is nothing, or at least something else. However, rest, the spaces of pause between productivity, can be an art in itself to learn.

In planning for study, it is important to plan for rest. This means factoring in a certain amount of downtime in your assessment of how long something is going to take you. The balance of rest and effort is ideally not weighed in large separate blocks of time, but rather peppered together in a natural rhythm. As in the old fable of the hare and the tortoise, slow and steady wins the race. Prolonged and consistent effort, with an early start, provides the conditions of mindful study that allow us to respond to our bodies and minds when rest is needed. Rather than delaying our start and then racing to the finish, we can slowly, peacefully, plod through the course of learning.

BE THERE NOW

When you are under pressure and studying regularly, you might find yourself feeling guilty when you are not at your desk. Developing a practice of being present and fully embracing wherever you are, whatever you are doing, means you can deeply and fully make the most of each opportunity. When you are studying, be there. When you are not studying and are doing something else, be there too. Learn to set aside any nagging concerns that you 'should' be back at your desk. If you never mentally leave your work, you will not get the break you need. Structure your study times around your lifestyle, leaving space for the things that are necessary to your own health, wellbeing and wider success as a human. It can be frustrating when you are doing something else, knowing you have a big exam or assignment to work on. But don't watch the clock thinking that precious hours are slipping by, wishing you could be at your desk. The value of each thing you choose to do is part of the greater picture of you.

The other activities we do that demand our attention can be just the sort of break from our learning that is necessary. Studies have shown that procrastination can be beneficial for study. It allows our minds space to simmer. While we seemingly occupy ourselves with other tasks, the brain is still quietly at work in the background. If we don't sometimes step away from the intense concentration of study, there is no time for the brain to brew and bubble up with new insight. However, procrastination is something you have to make time for. Anticipate that a period of sinking in is needed. Leave procrastination for the middle of your study, not the start.

EMBRACING REST

In surrendering to the body and mind's signals that rest is needed, we can respond with mindful awareness. Avoid shifting from one extreme to another. Don't swing on a pendulum from diligent student to sloth on the couch. In taking time to restore your energy and concentration, you can consciously experiment with efficient ways to revitalize yourself, rather than just clocking out as soon as you yawn. Stand up to close your eyes and take some deep breaths, stretch a little or put on a song and dance around the room. Set a time limit for your breaks and stick to them. If you can't develop a sense of trust with yourself by following through with your intention to return to your work, you may find you are less likely to allow yourself a break.

If you are taking a rest, don't make it like a walk around a prison yard, grey and dreary, only a few feet away from the incarceration of your study space. Our points of pause should be delightful punctuations that fill our souls with joy and pleasure. If you are stopping your study to shower, take a sweet-smelling bath with magnesium salts. If you are pausing for food, plate up something delicious and eat it away from your computer. Accepting that non-productivity is part of being productive can allow you to enjoy these moments fully and without reserve.

Practising rest in study is about practising for a healthy relationship with rest in your wider life. Learning to rest when you are a student, in a mindful way that is responsive to the unique needs of your body and mind, is an essential skill that you can carry forward into your future life.

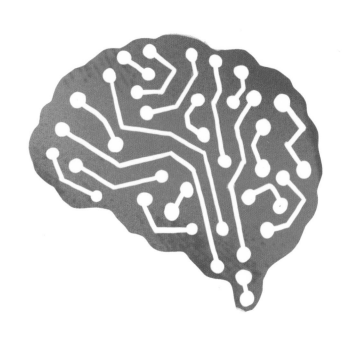

Technology &
Switching Off

Technology gives us the means to access a whole gamut of wonderful resources as students. But with this diversity comes a greater capacity for distraction. Unlike a book, which is a single-purpose piece of technology, a computer or tablet can have us flitting from one thing to another, or tripping into voids that draw our attention and keep us away from purposeful work. Contrary to popular belief, technology and mindfulness aren't incompatible. When we develop our skills in mindfulness, we can carry it with us everywhere, which includes the tricky terrain of notoriously addictive devices like phones, computers and tablets. Adopting mindful strategies that incorporate and moderate our use of technology is far more practical than trying to eradicate technology from our lives altogether.

The relationships we have with our devices are real. If you're anything like me, I feel like my life is contained in the grey-silver sandwich that is my laptop. But, as in every healthy partnership, we need to have some boundaries in place that reflect our needs and values. Too much of anything is bad for us. An awareness of self, which is at the core of a mindful approach, is an antidote for losing yourself in your technological device. Mindfulness can help us create a healthy balance.

MINDFUL PAUSES

Focus becomes increasingly difficult with the immediacy of technology. It seems every time I settle in to study, my phone rings or pings, an email pops up or a notification slides onto my screen. At times it feels like my devices are in competition for my attention. By habit, we spring to attention at their trills, answering the call, opening the email or clicking the notification. But there is space for hesitation here. Practise creating a small space for pause before automatically attending to technology's call. By allowing the briefest of moments to consider if you want to respond, you can shift your action from impulse reaction to considered choice. The important thing to bear in mind is that you have an option to decline, dismiss or postpone whatever it is that asks you for your attention.

We can also build an awareness around the length of time we spend on our screens. Take note of the time you start work, and consciously choose to get up regularly and stretch, have a walk or a drink of water. I make a point of not sitting at a screen for longer than 90 minutes at a time. Many devices have inbuilt tech to let you know when it's time for a break, but you can also use your own inbuilt timer, your body clock. Mindfully broaden your attention to internal and external markers of time – sensations of hunger or physical fatigue, the changing light outside

– and set the intention to pause regularly and shake off the virtual grasp. Technology can even assist us in our mindfulness practice through the many apps that are available. If you are already at your computer, why not incorporate a mindful meditation offered online as a break?

A MIRROR FOR THE MIND

Just as technology can influence our state of mind, it can also reflect it. Have you ever noticed how messy your computer desktop can become in the most demanding periods of learning? Don't even get me started on browsers! How many browser tabs or windows do you have open on your computer at this very moment? With multiple documents and countless windows perpetually open, how can we ever hope to find our focus?

When we take the time to clear and sort our virtual space, it tends to have a wonderful effect on how we are feeling and can help us regain our focus again.

Sweeping away unwanted documents and closing browsers has the effect of pruning the mind of loose ends. We attend to tasks that have been waiting for our attention and occupying vital mental space, and we discard projects that we probably weren't ever going to get around to. As we pay attention to the state of our virtual environments, we benefit our internal ones. The moments we take to bring order to our devices can be deeply calming when we do this with intention and awareness.

Technology is neither good nor bad. It has the capacity to make our lives and our work easier or harder. By staying aware and present, we can better moderate how we use technology for better rather than for worse. Incorporating mindfulness into our use of technology is like giving a torch to a hiker lost in the dark. Like the hiker, we need only the right tool to see our way and avoid falling down a rabbit hole.

When Life Gives You
Lemons

One of the greatest challenges that we face as students is how to keep our focus when we have challenges in our personal lives. Life can be a bumpy road. So often external stressors such as loss, grief and conflict will draw our attention and energy and leave us drained, both emotionally and mentally. Scholarship can feel superfluous when there are storms raging inside us.

Psychologist Abraham Maslow's hierarchy of needs theory acknowledges how difficult it is for us to self-actualize and become the most that we can be when we are experiencing setbacks in our relationships, personal security, employment, health or sense of self.

Life is unpredictable, and it is highly likely that every person on their study journey will be confronted with obstacles in these areas of their lives. Many students are just beginning their adult lives, trying to juggle finances, part-time jobs and romantic relationships, and learning to live away from their family. I remember during my first bachelor's degree, university was often the last thing on my mind. I was just trying to survive in the big wide world and, more often than not, floundering, sometimes even drowning a little.

Taking a sabbatical is one possibility if we are struggling, but mindfulness practices can help us so that we don't have to press pause to deal with the rest of our lives, because, life happens. The wheel keeps on turning. What we want is to have the tools to arm ourselves with, so that we can rise above our challenges and succeed despite the odds. Sometimes we don't have control over our external environment. Yet we can find ways to thrive on the inside through mindfulness, fostering a feeling of safety within that is grounded and secure.

RETURNING HOME

When we turn our attention inwards, we can find a
safe place, a home that we carry with us everywhere.
The earthy solidity of our body is always there for us,
ready to ground us. Our heightened emotions can be
planted in the damp and soothing soil of our quiet
selves. When we stop, close our eyes and breathe deeply,
checking in on each part of our bodies from head to
toe, we feel the stable weight and enduring strength
of our physical self and, at once, sense the ephemerality
of our fleeting conflicts and worries. By focusing on
the breath, and intentionally slowing its rhythm, we
can signal to the body that we are safe, and switch the
nervous system from fight or flight to rest and digest.
We become the rock, and our emotions the wind
which buffets against us. We can sink into ourselves
and remain grounded until the weather changes and
becomes calm again. This sort of grounding in the body
can be wonderful to do right before a presentation.
It can settle nerves and help focus the mind.

GRATITUDE: YIN & YANG

Gratitude practices are a powerful way to bring balance to our emotions. Just like yin and yang, there is always a light to the dark. The intensity of difficult situations and the emotions that accompany them can feel smothering, but if we take the time to sit quietly and bring our focus to the things we are grateful for, the shift in perspective can help to lift us out of darkness to see that even in the blackest of night skies there are stars. The more often and more consistently we mindfully tune into the positive aspects of our day-to-day lives, the more we begin to see them. These small yet powerful moments of focusing on what you are grateful for, perhaps the warmth of a cup of tea in our hands, the brightness of a sunny day or the support of a loving friend, equip us with a feeling of stability and can stand us in good stead through challenging times until we experience happier days.

Our intellectual growth and development can be the continuity that we lack in other aspects of our lives. I have been a student for the majority of my adult life.

While I have lived in many different houses, changed jobs numerous times, and had friends and loved ones come and go, my journey of learning has been an unbroken thread through my life. Step by step, we can walk through life's challenges, and still climb to the summit of our aspirations as students, so long as we can remain steady. Of course, when the wind of life whips ice-cold around us and the snow is deep, our steps may be slower, but if we keep on course, we will reach easier conditions and see the sun peep through the clouds again. The more we are able to stay on course, despite any setbacks, the greater our confidence will be in our ability to resiliently bounce back.

The Privilege
to Learn

It is a privilege to learn. Of course, this thought was far from my mind when I was a young girl, sitting in a hot and humid classroom. For much of my early education, I wanted to be somewhere else – indeed, my mind often *was* somewhere else. This I believe is incredibly common. In our adolescent years, our student minds are often somewhere else, occupied by other thoughts. We are more concerned for our social state, diverted by our friends and enemies in the jungle that is the classroom. It is no surprise that it can be difficult to focus on scholarship. As university students, life throws new challenges at us. On top of building new relationships, we may have to develop a newfound independence from our parents, work, share housing, cook and clean. For those of us who are students in adulthood, the demands of family, money, paid work and everyday life are difficult to juggle. Our attention and energy can seem endlessly disrupted, making the pursuit of study a relative tug-of-war for our minds.

It is never an easy path. In claiming that it is a privilege to be educated, I am not suggesting that it is always a golden experience. In many ways we could call it a white elephant gift – a rare elephant is undeniably precious, but it is a lot to take care of, and you can't just give it away. The practicalities of owning an elephant, like the practicalities of being a student, essentially boil down to it being a privilege that brings with it a lot of hard work. You could safely say that for the most part, being a student is far from fun. It can be stressful, confronting, exhausting and even at times painful. There is rarely growth, without some form of discomfort. But, if we can learn to be comfortable with a little discomfort, the rewards are great.

A GLOBAL PERSPECTIVE

In among the discomfort of learning there is a reality that we can hold close with mindful awareness: we are incredibly lucky to have the opportunity to learn. We need only look at psychologist Abraham Maslow's hierarchy of needs theory to see how many of our basic human requirements need to be fulfilled before we can climb to the lofty heights of the kind of self-actualization that comes with learning and the pursuit of expanding our knowledge and intellect. We first need to be physically safe, sheltered, nourished and cared for in an environment free from threats. We need to be accepted in a society that provides the foundation for learning, with our wellbeing taken care of. Only then can we turn our minds to more. For some people in the world, sadly, survival takes precedence over being a student.

It is a privilege to be able to learn. In the last few centuries there has been a significant shift in human learning. Education has become available to a far wider proportion of the population than just a minority of the global elite. It was only in recent history that women won the right to be educated, and there are still hundreds of millions of children around the world who don't have access to schooling. Cultivating a mindful awareness of the global reality of learning can provide a shift in perspective when our close-up existence becomes uncomfortable. It can be all too easy to lose our motivation in the day-to-day grind. But if, from time to time, we can situate those realities in a broader perspective, we can temper our experience of student life with gratitude that we are even here, and gratitude for those moments when the heat is turned up and we need to sweat it out.

ZOOM OUT

When we widen our frame of reference to perceive our present selves within a broader global context, we can see our situation with greater clarity. In the times when you feel dissatisfied with being a student, draw your focus mindfully to where you are, seated in a classroom perhaps, and then try zooming out a little, to your college or university, then a little further, to your town, your state, your country, and then finally to the whole planet. Contemplate where you are in a wider context and you might find a clearer perspective of how lucky you really are to be able to learn.

When we give our attention to what is happening around us, we can influence what is happening within us. In taking the time to zoom out and contemplate a broader view of our learning, we can bring to mind the deeper, far-reaching benefits of our study. Learning can open new pathways in our lives, enrich our perspective on life, and provide us with the joy and delight of discovery and the satisfaction of acquiring new knowledge of ourselves and the world around us.

Students of
Life

If we do it right, we will be students for the entirety of
our lives. But doing it right doesn't mean always aceing
our exams and topping the class. It is, rather, walking a
path in which we find the joy of learning, of building
knowledge, competency and confidence. We have a
limitless potential for growth and discovery which
makes it possible to continue learning, formally or
informally, throughout our lives, if we can but enjoy
the process. Many might say that they do not enjoy or
have not enjoyed being a student. This is a terrible loss.
Mindfulness is a path to finding our joy in learning.

One of the great pleasures of learning is being able
to experience our knowledge in practice. What was

once hard, becomes automatic and effortless, and with competence grows confidence. But because the challenge of not knowing something is invariably so much more prominent in our minds than the ease of knowing something, we don't always notice how far we have come. There is an infinite amount of learning that we have all done that we don't celebrate or even notice every day. Take eating, for instance. When you were a year old, you probably ended up with food all over your face when you tried to feed yourself, but now you have that skill so well handled you don't even think about it. Knowledge applied can be a source of delight if you can only bring your awareness to it. From time to time, reflect on how your studies have equipped you to do things that you would never have been able to do otherwise. This self-awareness is vital if you are going to tap into the joy of learning. Being able to reflect on your successes and acknowledge your progress will help you foster the ability to persevere.

A BEGINNING, NOT AN ENDING

When people finish their academic study, I often hear statements like, 'Well, I'm never going to study again!' It is as though, now they have reached their goal of attaining a qualification, they hope to never set eyes on a textbook again. I understand there is some cause for celebration that you are no longer required to be scrutinized by assessment, rated and marked by your teachers, but just because you gain a qualification, it doesn't mean you should stop learning. The rigors of institutionalized study will have empowered you to learn independently, equipping you with the tools of enquiry to lead your own pursuit of knowledge, directed simply by an inquisitive mind. Finishing at college or university simply means the training wheels are off, so why not take your newly minted mind out for another expedition, one that is entirely designed and led by you? Seeing yourself as a life-long learner, not a student who has reached their conclusion, is vital if you are to take up the helm of growth and learning once again.

Mindfulness is typified by an attitude of curiosity. There are any number of questions that pop into our minds that can lead us to new places of discovery. When we take time for stillness or even practise mindfulness on the go, where we are present and aware of our mental dialogue, we can catch these questions and natural curiosities as they drift in and out of our consciousness. These little gems are what sets us on a path in pursuit of treasure. When you observe yourself questioning something, head to the library, or pick up your phone and follow that thread of enquiry instead of flicking through social media.

LEARNING COMMUNITIES

Part of the reason why I love to learn is that I surround myself with a community of like-minded people who are interested in the same things as me. Too many people go through life wishing they could learn to make pottery or draw or play a musical instrument but do nothing about it. When we are in tune with ourselves and listen in to our deepest desires, we will find ample opportunity for a life of learning. Take music lessons, learn to cha cha, volunteer to go on an archeological dig, take flying lessons. Being a student doesn't mean sitting in a lecture theatre – it could be taking to the stage and learning to sing opera. When we follow our joy, we meet others who are doing the same thing, and we build communities of friends based on a love of life-long learning.

Growth is the antidote for decay. When we are mindful, seeking opportunities to learn with curiosity and wonder, we stay young and vigorous. We provide ourselves with the ongoing opportunity to cultivate and understand ourselves, in the process of becoming all we hope we can be. Being a mindful and life-long learner is walking through life with curiosity, wonder and a passion to understand more. Learn your whole life long, and you will live a rich life.

ACKNOWLEDGEMENTS

I wish to dedicate this book to my Dad and my Husband. From a young age, Dad reinforced the importance of self-belief and setting clear goals, but above all, of enjoying the journey. He emphasized living gratefully and this influenced me to be a person who always sees the positive. Thanks to him, I have a strong awareness of the simple things we can celebrate every day. I am so lucky to have such a wonderful role model, teacher and Father.

To my life partner, Edgar Choy. You have taught me how to be still, to be slow, and to relish pleasure and fun. You always encourage me to temper my fiery passion for learning with the softer energy of yin, urging me to rest, relax and laugh. You gently guide me to balance, to find the softness in mindfulness, ever directing me to the art of listening to my body and responding lovingly to its needs.